POST INDUST NATION
(COLLECTED POEMS)

So she sent him off to the army,
"See what you can do with this brat!"
They put him in a fancy suit
And told him he might not come back.

He fought the wars in Yugoslavia,
Went down to Tripoli.
Got wounded in Armenia
Sailed across the Caspian Sea.

His mother sat in a council flat,
Her hands wrapped round her head.
Praying for God's forgiveness
Hoping he wouldn't come back dead.

Another mental breakdown,
A bottle of gin by her side.
Pills for manic depression,
That the doctor had prescribed.

She's been clinging to a precipice,
Waiting for a rescue team.
Wrapped up in her blanket,
Lost within a dream.

This destined fate comes fast,
And time will never stand still.
She wished that she could edit her past,
And never came off the pill.

Now she's waiting for that rescue team,
But it never will arrive.
The only thing that's certain,
Is her son is not alive.

Albion, old Albion,
You sent our sons to war.
But the glory turns to grief,
When it comes knocking at your door.

7.   YORK HALL, BETHNAL GREEN.

The match had been made.
And no doubt
Of my mentors decision.
I squat,
Knees to chest,
And wait for the ending.
Here,
I have concealed,
And shut up apart.
My opponent avoided.
I step on the scales,
Hoping somehow,
To fail the weight.
Or maybe the doctor,
Will deny me.

The match had been made.

No doubts, I tell myself.
For here I am,
In the hall of dreams.
Where fighters have climbed,
Into the blood stained ring.
I leave behind the fear;
Kit bags,
Towels,
Good luck charms.
And those who wait in turn
To climb under the ropes,

Are polite with their nervous smiles.
But nothing can hide,
The sense of distress.

The match had been made.

Time to prepare.
Hold out my hands,
In silence.
I give in.
Acceptance.
In clinical crepe,
My hands are wrapped.
And then pushing down,
Into claustrophobic cushions.
The smell,
Of stale damp leather;
Laced,
Now taped and imprisoned,
Too late for escape.

The match had been made

Then dance away, find space.
Jab, parry...
Uppercut, right cross, left hook.
Remember...
Throw a right,
Come back with a hook.
Remember...

Hands up! Hands up!
And the pads are held,
To hasten me on.
Prepare me to capitulate,
Accept the violence,
Be the stronger,
To please and excite.

The match had been made.

Now the call.
The rush of the walk.
Amongst the cheers and shouts,
The blanket of smoke.
The stench of beer,
Then under the ropes.
The resin box,
Step forward, shake hands.
Now silence; bright light,
Red to blue,
I await the bell.
Just two stand tall
To fight in the glory,
Of the famous York Hall.

The match had been made.

I shall not accept this fatalism,
Or the nightmares that torture me.
As I lie in my bed,
I dream of life,
Beneath the fountain of blood...
Crimson red.

Stephen Hindley (21.06.1985)

11. PINK FLOYD CIRCUS BLUES

It was a momentary lapse of reason,
A singularly second delay.
Syd Barrett refused to move his lips,
Whilst miming to 'See Emily Play.'
And all those years I spent,
Trying to work out these confusing clues,
Careful with that axe Eugene,
Yeah man...It's the Pink Floyd Circus Blues.

Atom Heart Mother,
The Dark Side of the Moon.
An allusion to lunacy,
And a twenty minute tune.
Roger on an ego trip,
Sitting high up on The Wall.
Gerald Scarfe puppets,
Twenty five feet tall.

These songs were on a parallel,
Between politics and Animal Farm.
Self-inflicted bodily damage,
And needless mental harm.
There's someone in my head,
My God, I've got nothing to lose.
It's a simple case of brain damage,
Yeah man...The Pink Floyd Circus Blues.

Pink Anderson,
Floyd Council,
Candy and a current bun.
Songs with little reason,
Made up for a bit of fun.
Money making con...
Wish That You Were Here.
The times they are a changing Bob,
The only daughter of the engineer.

Two hundred million records,
But I still think they got it wrong.
After all, it's supposed to be music...
It's only a bloody song.
And now there's the Endless River,
A Big Spliff and a final cruise.
Meddle, The Wall, Final Cut,
Yeah man...The Pink Floyd Circus Blues.

12.   HATE BEING ME (sometimes)

I was in a happy mood one spring day,
Smiling, shining, on my way.
Then under the bridge I walked;
Thinking about all the things I'd done,
And what a horrible person I'd become.

Slumped in a corner at half past three,
A belly full of beer I can hardly see.
Worst for wear and I've lost my key,
Sometimes I just hate being me.

Meeting with people I don't even like,
Taking the piss 'cos they're not my type.
It's not my fault that they can't see,
That sometimes I just hate being me.

Showing my grief when I don't even care,
You lose someone close and it doesn't seem fair.
Life's a bitch and it don't come free,
Sometimes I just hate being me.

I think of myself I don't think of you,
I only do things I want to do.
I don't want to change so just let it be,
Sometimes I just hate being me.

Why do I argue that wrong is right?
Why make you cry half the night.
Am I so blind that I can't see?
Sometimes I just hate being me.

Why do I shout black and blue?
About things that never concern you.
Why can't I relax laid back and free,
Sometimes I just hate being me.

Why do I never ask any questions?
Show no interest offer no suggestions.
Look at my face because I can't see,
Why you would want to be like me.

13. HOME SWEET HOME

Rainy nights.
This one in particular.
A drive along the motorway home,
and rain hitting down on the windscreen,
Making it difficult to see.
So I tucked into the slow lane,
and plodded on at a steady fifty,
Keeping space in front of me.
Making it feel
like I'm the only person on this road;
Someone once told me,
It was the busiest road in Europe.

And then,
The single transporter.
With the pink Chevrolet,
sitting comfortably,
and overtaking me slowly...
So I could just turn my head,
and watch the whole thing sail pass,
And cut right in front of me;
Then...
Moving off slowly,
opening a space that was mine,
just a few moments ago.
And then my motorway became my freeway,
and I was dreaming,
All the way along route 66,
through the night;
With the rain hitting my windscreen;

And me,
Behind that pink Chevrolet.

Then suddenly,
Unconsciously;
Here I am,
Turning the corner,
Into the avenue and past the bend,
Where the two James boys
Had smashed their car so badly,
Where they were thrown into the street,
Not knowing anything about their deaths.

And the flowers now waiting,
To be removed and incinerated.
No longer a loving and tearful reminder
Of lost youth,
But more about time and decay.
And there it was;
A short journey home.
From where it doesn't matter.
To home...
Home Sweet Home.

14. I HATE THE FUCKING COTSWOLDS

Sycamore tree,
Village green.
Residents,
Rarely seen.
Privet hedge,
Lonely pub,
I hate the fucking Cotswolds!

Empty fields,
Grey stone.
4X4's,
Second home.
Riding boots,
Barbour coat.
I hate the fucking Cotswolds!

Campsites,
Shower block.
Two toilets,
No lock.
Heavy rain,
Never again.
I hate the fucking Cotswolds!

Picture postcard,
Tourist trap.
Day trippers,
Buying CRAP.
Cream teas,
I'm never going back,
'Cos I hate the fucking Cotswolds!

15. NORTH EASTERN SHORE

We stood there,
Side by side.
Together watching out...
Out, over the beach.
And during low tide,
The beach grew wider.
And it stretched far; until it met the mass,
Of concrete and steel.
We stood there,
Side by side.
And we studied the derelict colliery.
Its wheel a solemn testimony;
Echoing the poignant extinction,
Of a once proud community.

Figures bent double,
Moving in time.
Grey hanging figures,
On a grey landscape line.
Men picking coal,
From the wet muddy floor,
Of the dreary despairing,
North Eastern Shore.

So you sit in the indifferent chair,
flick the coin and watch it spin.
It always turns tails up,
and heads; it will never win.
What protracted your willing youth?
the strong athletic frame?
Not age or growing adversity,
but by playing the cautious game.

Same time,
Same distance,
Same shit.

18. BISCUIT

The English have a tradition,
That they have with a cup of tea.
A variety of assorted biscuits,
And there're never sugar free.

Now I've travelled the whole world over,
I'm a laid back travelling man.
I ate curries in Calcutta,
And Sushi in Japan.

I ate Paella in Valencia,
From the back of my camper van.
Toad in the hole in Yorkshire,
Baklava in Kurdistan.

Tried buttered scones in Devon,
The cream was very thick.
Ate Eccles cake in Lancaster,
The pastry made me sick.

Aloo Chat and Katchori,
Karinto and Wasabi peas.
Turkish delight and Nuns Puff's,
I ate all of these.

But one thing I could never get,
Was a crispy fox's cream.
Or a yummy jammy dodger,
They were never found or seen.

Give big issue seller, a cynical look.
She'll waste all that money,
Loose change that she took.
She'll spend it on drugs,
And fuck up her life.
You don't really care,
'cos you're not very nice.

She just wants to talk,
To you and me.
Not hear the sound,
Of sweet charity.
It's easy to give,
Don't expect something back.
Spend time together,
And get on her track.

21. T.V. DINNER

T.V. they say,
Brings us closer to reality.
Images thrown,
Into comfortable sitting rooms.
T.V. dinners,
In front of death.

That child I saw,
A girl.
Not more than five years old.
Lying face upwards,
With arms spread,
Arranged in cruciform.
A white sheet,
Draped to conceal horror.
The filthy sucking mud,
Allaying its grief.
A fly, exploring the lifeless head.

That child,
I see lying dead,
Makes me think of my own,
Lying safe and warm,
In bed.
I feel sad,
Hurt.
Angry.
This is a forty minute,
Documented emotion.
Tomorrow...
Will I forget?

22. TAX

I didn't see it coming,
It was like a bolt out of the blue.
Lights that used to shine,
Had faded ...
Dulled, suffocated,
No longer strong and new.

Take a moment to think,
And cast back over the years.
The meteoric rise, like climbing...
The treacherous mountain,
Ascending,
Without fear.

It was a confrontation,
And a shock.
It could kill, although expected.
Blunt, callous, text and numbers,
The dreaded New Year,
And the arrival of the tax bill.

23. THE BOARDING PARTY

I fell...
A four foot drop,
Landing face down.
Damp, well worn steamers,
Laced tightly to my feet.
Rogues Yarn,
Pushing into my face.
I felt sick.

In seconds we hurried,
Dressed to kill.
And we grouped...
Our posts taken,
Then informed.
The enemy had struck amidships.
Rammed,
And ripped a hole twenty foot.

At the magazine,
I took my gun.
Ready to fight and kill,
Or die.
A pitch black night,
Our boarding party stood.
All holding our balance,
While the ship tossed and rolled.

Cold and petrified,
All twelve we stood.
In the wind and mighty roar,
Of the strong force eight.
And as the sea summoned,
I heard Dylan sing:
"All you seasick sailors rowing home,
It's all over now baby blue."

24. TRENCH

I could see into,
And beyond those eyes.
The saddened eyes of time,
Wrinkled by life's bitter struggle.
The misery and pain,
Have taken their toll.
Yet my eyes met yours,
With a sense of recognition.
'Tell me old man,
Where did we meet?'
Was it in our youthful days?
When time stood still.

Did we run together as children?
Our young hearts sharing innocence.
As if all beauty,
In our unknown and forbidden world,
Danced and laughed,
At our unspoilt plight.
Or was it when we stood together,
Our innocence stripped,
Our minds suppressed and mocked,
Thoughts examined and primed.
I remember those eyes,
Locked deep into my own.

I've got tracksuit bottoms,
To change into at night.
A ten year old t-shirt,
Getting smaller and tight.
I keep thinking that maybe,
I should clean myself up.
It's the mid-life crisis,
And I'm stuck in a rut.

I'm going to bed at night,
At half past nine.
A couple of beers,
And a bottle of wine.
I wake up in the morning,
And check my body parts.
I've got the mid-life crisis,
And another day starts.

I like to listen to jazz
On the radio
I wanna be cool
Give radio one a go.
But there's only so much
That I can take.
I've got the mid life-crisis,
And I've got a head ache.

My dress sense in fashion
Is getting pretty insane.
I refuse to wear old clothes
Conservative and plain.
You won't find streetwear
In Marks and Sparks.
Full of old farts,
It's a mid-life crisis.

I'm weighing myself,
Three times a day.
Convincing myself,
That I look O.K.
But my body condition,
Ain't what it used to be,
I've got the mid-life crisis,
'''''''''''''Vanity.

So tell me my friend,
When will it end?
This mid-life crisis
Is driving me round the bend.
One day I'll just give up,
And fade away.
Until then I'll just learn,
To live for the day.

Try a book, end the week...
Too tired to go to sleep.
History lesson, been and gone,
Forget the past, the futures long.

Mahatma Ghandi, where's my coat,
Men of peace, now there's a joke.
Iraq, Iran, Afghanistan,
U.S.A. or U.K.

Multi-cultural, multi-lingual,
What's the deal, it's not that simple.
Pop culture, Pop music,
Here it is, but you don't choose it.

So how's your life?
So how's your life?
So how's your life that you live now?

29. EMBRACE

Help me subscribe,
To this multi-cultural society.
I want to embrace other cultures,
And share diversity.
I don't want to live under the shadow,
Of the stars and stripes.
Restrict our freedom,
And remove our rights.

I don't want to be threatened,
By a suicide bomb.
Or take my revenge,
Through someone else's son.
I don't want to be subjected,
To the war on terror.
I'm terrified,
It's going to last forever.

I don't want to be offended,
Every day.
By people who expect,
I should see things their way.
Hate of Paki's and Poles,
Muslims and Jews.
I don't want to hear incessant,
Right wing views.

I don't want to be filled,
With hate and rage.
Be put in a corner,
Or held in a cage.
I don't want to be subjected,
To the war on terror.
I'm terrified,
It's going to last forever.

30. BLOODY DISGRACE

My god I've lost it again,
My mobile phone went missing.
I was searching around,
Like a stupid fool,
For my fully dependent,
Modern tool.
On my hands and knees like a stubborn mule,
When my mobile phone went missing.

I thought I'd better phone the phone,
But the phone I'm phoning is me.
I'm still searching around to answer,
The bloody answer machine.
I even thought to leave a message,
Well what a stupid thing to do.
I checked all the cupboards,
But I didn't have a clue.

Well I spent all morning thinking,
About that bloody phone.
I've got my life programmed in it,
And without it I'm all alone.
I had all my numbers stored,
My credit cards as well.
Bank balance, loans,
Everything as far as I could tell.

I've had it with this modern life,
It wasn't just the phone.
I tried to clean the satellite dish,
One night when I got home.
There's no signal now,
And I want to have a moan.
But I can't even do that,
'Cos I can't find my fucking phone.

I just had to come to terms with my life,
So I took a walk into town.
Met a strange looking woman
 Who tried to calm me down.
"Just put it down to your age,
take it easy," she said.
"Enjoy life young man,
'cos one day you'll be dead."

"Try to give up the romance,
of a younger life.
You gotta control your rage,
You gotta try to be nice.
And when you forget things,
Just try to be cool,
And don't run around like a headless fool"

I could see her point,
When she spoke.
This stressful life,
Just aint a joke.
But her friendly advice,
Didn't mean much to me,
'Cos I got my life planned out,
Predictably...
You see.

So I turned my back,
And carried on down the road.
Taking with me,
My heavy load.
That woman kept me thinking about things,
For days and days.
But it's hard to make changes,
When you're stuck in your ways.

Maybe I should take these blinkers off,
And have a good look around.
Stand up straight,
Stop crawling around on the ground.
I got it pretty cushy you know,
Maybe I need a slap in the face.
Get myself sorted out,
It's a bloody disgrace.

31. AMBULANCE

I didn't think that it could happen.
I never saw beyond my easy world.
Sitting here,
Who am I crying for?
I felt so lonely once you closed the door.

I glanced at you as you ran the lights,
You could have been my own flesh and blood.
But while you claimed the streets for your own,
My world was changing,
I felt so alone.

Was god with me in time and space?
I couldn't imagine one hour ago.
Thinking about all the consequence,
All the things I had to say...
It made no sense.

We woke that morning with the same sky,
And you came to me just like a song.
Now here we are on a journey.
The whole world stops;
To take you home.

Sanctify this journey and clear the path ahead.
The angels we believe in, will lead you to your bed.
This was a crossroad, I knew had to come.
It was I who held your hand,
It was me, I was the one.

32. ENSURE PLUS

I'll have another Ensure Plus,
Milk shake to make you fat.
Fortified vitamins and proteins,
Banana flavour is where it's at.
No sudden weight loss for me,
I need to pile on the pounds.
A bottle contains 300 calories,
And it's not half as bad as it sounds.

I lots my taste at three weeks,
And alarm bells started to ring.
The red cheeks, the sore mouth,
And my tongue was starting to sting.
I was flattened by the chemo,
Spent two days lying in bed.
Worrying about my weight loss,
Ensure Plus, swimming round my head.

Drifting in and out of sleep,
Darkness turning to light.
Forging dreams of hopefulness,
Nazareth comes fresh and bright.
And the victims I met yesterday,
Share the path that we have to take.
Drink another bottle of Ensure Plus,
The 300 calorie super milk shakes.

Doctors and nurses,
And God I trust.
Thank you for giving me,
Ensure Plus.

33. épée d'espoir

St. Raphael came to me one night
and smiled.
He lay comfort to my pain,
I was never prepared.

The next day I awoke
and I felt warmth.
It flowed through my veins.
Treatment is solitary.

My head was caged,
Imprisoned.
Surrendered to the machine.
Relinquished.

Sometimes I felt like losing my mind,
But faith kept me strong.
From my bed I heard the song;
"Hang on to your dream"

The beaches stretch wide and far,
The nightlife cold and damp.
And if you need to isolate,
There's plenty of room to camp.
From the Midlands to the North,
Cleveland and the Yorkshire Dales;
If you want another language,
Then cross the border into Wales.

From the East Coast to the West,
An island surrounded by sea.
No need to visit Europe anymore,
We're self-sufficient and totally free.
Spend holidays in England's glory,
Roast dinners and warm beer.
I've never been to Blackpool;
To ride the carousel on the coastal pier.

38. RETURN

There are no rules
meters, sonnets or rhymes.
Free verse echoes life
and re-awakens old times.

Recovery extinguishes
fear of a boundary line.
Of long valued obsessions,
sequence, structure, design.

Discover the dark secrets
of the clear celestial sphere.
The early morning chorus,
Awakes; enchants the ear.

No clock to glance
or season; bid farewell.
Time is not allowed to yield,
or arrest your soul to sell.

39. THE POET

Listen...
Listen to my poem.
Hear this story,
this story for you.
I ask you to listen,
just once.

I can see how it can take you,
grab you,
control you,
wake you at any time
and send your mind,
into whirlpools of dizziness.
And all this,
when minutes earlier,
you were absolute.

My frantic notes,
less you forget.
But so clear,
as fresh spring water.
One thought on top of another.
Layers that comfort,
like a warm blanket.
Layers that question,
and torment.

Listen,
Listen to my poem.

Her poem was like a song.
It had rhythm,
rhyme and BEAT.
You know...
I took in every word.
Desired, ate and swallowed.
I was left with something.
Somehow,
she had touched my soul.

40. AFTERWORD

Make the world a better place,
Come up with a good idea.
It's amazing what you can think up,
In a week, a month or a year.
Write a song, join a club,
Go swimming in the sea.
Remember you only have one life,
Be happy, kind and free.

Acknowledgements

To my family and the NHS who helped me get through the worst period of my life. Thanks to Alliance Publishing Press for making this book possible.